WINTER SPORTS

SNOWBOARDING

Paul Mason

Raintree is an imprint of Capstone Global Library Limited, a company incorporated in England and Wales having its registered office at 7 Pilgrim Street, London, EC4V 6LB – Registered company number: 6695582

To contact Raintree please phone 0845 6044371, fax + 44 (0) 1865 312263, or email myorders@ raintreepublishers.co.uk. Customers from outside the UK please telephone +44 1865 312262.

Text © Capstone Global Library Limited 2014
First published in hardback in 2014
The moral rights of the proprietor have been asserted.

Edited by Adam Miller, Nancy Dickmann, and John-Paul Wilkins
Designed by Richard Parker and Ken Vail Graphic Design
Picture research by Elizabeth Alexander
Originated by Capstone Global Library Ltd
Production by Vicki Fitzgerald
Printed and bound in China by Leo Paper Products Ltd

ISBN 978 1 406 26033 5
17 16 15 14 13
10 9 8 7 6 5 4 3 2 1

British Library Cataloguing in Publication Data
Mason, Paul
Snowboarding. – (Winter Sports)
A full catalogue record for this book is available from the British Library.

Acknowledgements
We would like to thank the following for permission to reproduce photographs: Alamy pp. 6 (© Andrey Artykov), 39 (© AF archive); Alli Sports p. 23; Corbis pp. 5, 14 (© John G. Mabanglo/ epa/), 8, 11 (© Ocean), 10 (© Atsushi Tomura/ Aflo/Aflo), 12 (© Radius Images), 15 (© Sampics), 17 (© Erich Schlegel), 20 (© Troy Wayrynen/ NewSport), 25 (© Aurelien Meunier/Icon SMI), 29 (© Robert Parigger/epa), 33 (© Paul Cunningham); Getty Images pp. 4 (Agence Zoom), 7 (Johannes Kroemer), 9 (Jean-Pierre Clatot/AFP), 13 (Jared Alden), 16 (Nicholas Ratzenboeck/AFP), 18, 21, 24, 31, 40 (Doug Pensinger), 19 (Adrian Dennis/ AFP), 22 (Jed Jacobsohn), 26 (Richard Bord), 28 (Jonathan Nackstrand/AFP), 30, 32, 35 (Fabrice Coffrini/AFP), 36 (Getty for Pepsi Inc), 38 (Mark Ralston/AFP), 41 (Alexandra Beier/Bongarts); Newscom p. 27 (Mathieu Belanger/Reuters); Press Association Images p. 37 (Christian murdock/ AP); Shutterstock pp. imprint page (© IM_photo), 34 (Lucas Kane / Aurora Open), 44 (© Marcel Jancovic).

Design features reproduced with permission of Shutterstock (© donatas1205, © elena moiseeva, © Triff, © 2happy, © David M. Schrader, © Christian Musat, © Vishnevskiy Vasily, © idea for life, © Ana de Sousa, © Konstantin Shishkin, © David M. Schrader, © ilolab, © Lizard, © javarman).

Cover photo of a snowboarder jumping reproduced with permission of Corbis (© Mike Powell).

Every effort has been made to contact copyright holders of material reproduced in this book. Any omissions will be rectified in subsequent printings if notice is given to the publisher.

CONTENTS

Some words are shown in bold, **like this**. You can find out what they mean by looking in the glossary.

THE EDGE OF DISASTER

The date: 17 February 2006

The place: Olympic snowboard cross course, Bardonecchia, Italy

The riders line up, ready for the first ever Olympic snowboard cross final. One of them is Lindsey Jacobellis of the United States. Jacobellis is the hot favourite. She has already won two world championships, and has looked almost unbeatable during this competition.

The starting signal goes, and Jacobellis builds a big lead. Her turns, jumps, and landings are just within the limits of control. Jacobellis's closest rival is the Swiss rider Tanja Frieden, but heading into the last-but-one jump, Frieden is 3 seconds behind. Jacobellis starts to relax – and that's when disaster strikes.

Jacobellis gets off to a flying start, as Dominique Maltais of Canada trails behind.

LINDSEY JACOBELLIS

Born: 19 August 1985
From: Connecticut, USA
Job: Professional snowboarder

Jacobellis is most famous for her crash in the 2006 Winter Olympics, but she *should* be known as one of the best female snowboard cross racers ever. By 2012, she had won 4 world championships, 25 world cup races, and – of course – an Olympic silver medal.

"Snowboarding's meant to be fun. I was just having fun."

– *Lindsey Jacobellis neatly sums up snowboarding, in which having a good time is as important as winning*

Snowboarders sometimes make their jumps more stylish by adding twists, **spins**, and even **flips**. With a massive lead, Jacobellis decides to add a bit of style to her last jump. As she takes off, she twists the board sideways and grabs the edge. Coming in to land she lets go, straightens it up, catches the edge of the board in the snow – and crashes. Frieden whizzes past to win the gold medal, and Jacobellis limps across the line for silver.

Never let anyone tell you that snowboarding isn't exciting!

A (LITTLE) BIT OF HISTORY

Snowboards developed from crazy-looking devices called Snurfers. Snurfers appeared in the 1960s. They were like a short, fat, super-wide ski, which you stood on while sliding downhill. A rope was tied to the nose for balance and control – but there wasn't *much* control, and crashes were common.

The "swallowtail" board first appeared in 1972, and is still in production today.

Snurfer to snowboard

In 1977, a young Snurfer rider called Jake Burton modified his Snurfer so that his feet were attached to the deck. It gave him more control over turns and jumps. Soon Burton was making a new kind of board, like a giant wooden skateboard deck with waterski foot **bindings**. During the 1980s designs like Burton's developed into the modern snowboard.

Snowboarding takes off

Snowboarding became more and more popular. For skateboarders and surfers, it was a fantastic alternative sport. Skiers saw how much fun the snowboarders were having, and gave it a try. By 2004, there were over six million snowboarders.

NO WAY!

It seems crazy now, but in the 1980s fewer than 1 in 10 ski resorts allowed snowboarding. At most of those, you had to take a skills test before going out on the slopes.

JAKE BURTON CARPENTER

Born: 29 April 1954
From: New York City, USA
Job: Snowboard businessman

Known as Jake Burton, he started making snowboards in the 1970s. Few people bought them, partly because they were thought too expensive at around £24! But Burton Snowboards continued, and today his company is the world's biggest snowboard manufacturer.

BASICS

The basics of snowboarding haven't changed much since the early days. All you need is a board, bindings, and boots. Of course, not everyone enjoys exactly the same type of snowboarding, so it's lucky there are different styles. The two basic ones are freestyle and freeride.

Freestyle

Freestyle riders love to throw in tricks – **aerials**, **grinds**, and other moves inspired by skateboarding – whenever they get a chance. Freestylers often head straight for the snow park, where ramps and other obstacles have been built to make a kind of skatepark on snow. Or they might head for the half-pipe (find out more about this on pages 22–25). Really, though, you can freestyle anywhere. The best riders use natural ramps, lumps of snow, fallen trees, or even walls as the starting point for tricks.

An **off-piste** rider goes large with a big aerial in Japan.

Freeride

If free*style* is inspired by skateboarding, free*riding* is closer in spirit to surfing or downhill mountain biking. There are fewer jumps and tricks, and each **run** usually lasts longer. Freeriders especially love to get out in fresh **powder** and carve deep turns all the way down a big slope.

"I live for those powder days. I love being in the mountains. I love being out there. I love snowboarding. To me there's nothing better."

– James Stentiford, UK pro snowboarder and freerider

JAMES STENTIFORD

Born: 1 November 1971
From: Braunton, Devon, UK
Job: Pro snowboarder

Stentiford is an extreme sports allrounder who surfs, skateboards, kiteboards, and rides a mountain bike. He regularly features in DVDs, and competes on the World Freeride Tour.

Clothing

The basic clothing for snowboarding is really simple. You need warm, water-resistant clothes that don't make you sweaty when you get hot.

JACKET
Water-resistant and breathable. Most have thin, fleecy insulation inside. Snow skirt keeps out snow if you fall and slide down the slope.

HELMET
Protects head in crashes and collisions.

GOGGLES
Prevent eyes from watering at high speed and protect them from light reflecting off snow. Come with different lenses for sunshine or low-light conditions.

GLOVES
Should be warm, waterproof, and **breathable**.

FLEECE
In cold conditions most riders wear a fleece; if it's really cold, some even add a **gilet**.

TROUSERS
Water-resistant and breathable, they may have extra-thick fabric on the bottom, for sitting on snow.

BASE LAYER
Thermal base layer moves sweat away from the skin, keeping snowboarders warm and dry.

	FREESTYLE	FREERIDE
Board	Shorter (up to the rider's chin when stood on end) and the same shape at both ends	Longer (to the rider's nose when stood on end) and longer at the front than the back
Boots	More flexible, to make tricks such as spins and aerials easier	Stiffer, which makes high-speed turns and control easier and less painful
Bindings	Lower at the back and less stiff, again to help make tricks easier	Higher at the back and stiffer to aid with turns and control

Equipment

All any snowboarder really needs is a board, comfortable boots, and bindings. The equipment is slightly different for freestyle and freeriding, but you can use a freestyle board for freeriding, and vice versa.

Binding

Boot

Board

BASIC SKILLS

The basic skills in snowboarding are steering/turning the board, adjusting your speed, stopping, and catching lifts.

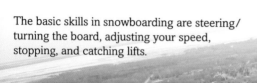

This snowboarder is goofy, riding right-foot-first down the hill.

Are you regular or goofy?

The first thing a beginner snowboarder has to decide is whether they ride **regular** or **goofy**. Regulars ride with their left foot forward, goofys with their right. One guide to what you will be is to kick a ball. Whichever foot you naturally kick with usually goes at the back of the snowboard.

Starting off

Standing on a snowboard for the first time is a wobbly experience. You need to keep your knees bent and your weight low down. Then, facing the snow and with the board across the slope (NOT pointing downhill!), you stand up. Digging the **toe edge** into the snow holds the board in place.

Putting a bit of extra weight on your front foot starts the board sliding to the side. Removing the extra weight slows and stops the board.

Ski lifts can be awkward and uncomfortable for snowboarders. When there is no footbar, some snowboarders rest their board on the opposite foot.

Catching lifts

Chairlifts are easiest for beginner snowboarders to use. When you join the queue, take your back foot out of its binding and use it to shuffle or **skate** the board forward. As the lift approaches, bend your knees slightly and point the nose of your board uphill. When the lift is right behind you, sit down on it. Once you are sitting comfortably, lower the safety bar. If there is a footbar, you can rest the board on it.

Turning and stopping

The next step is to turn onto the board's **heel edge**. Start on an easy, wide slope. Crouching low, you turn to look over your forward shoulder, in the direction you want to turn. Your shoulders, arms, and hips all twist in the same direction, and the board follows along, turning with you. Once you have the basic turn down, you can try carving (see page 15).

NO WAY!

In 1995, Mads Jonsson of Norway set a world record for the longest snowboard jump ever. He soared 57 metres (187 feet). That would have been enough to jump most football pitches!

13

ADVANCED SKILLS

NO WAY!

Snowboard tricks have some crazy names: the bloody Dracula, chicken salad, mule kick, roast beef, and Swiss cheese, are just a few examples!

Advanced snowboard skills are the techniques you see riders using in competitions. At the very top level, they need to be able to do them smoothly and stylishly.

Aerials

There are hundreds of different types of aerial. Riders add difficulty and style using:

- Spins – A full spin around is called a 360, because the rider spins through 360 degrees.

- Flips – A head-over-heels tumble in the air, done either backwards or forwards.

- **Grabs** – A grab is when the rider holds on to part of the board while in the air.

Tricks are harder if they are started **switch**. That means riding backwards, with the tail of the board in front.

BAM! If you're going to try tough tricks, you have to be ready for the odd crash to happen!

14

Slides

Slides are done on obstacles such as rails and boxes. In competition, you mostly see them in slopestyle (see pages 26 and 27). Many slides were inspired by skateboard moves.

Carving turns

In a carving turn, the snowboard does not slide sideways. Instead, the whole turn is done with the metal edge of the board biting into the snow. Carving turns are great for:

a) Throwing up an impressive spray of snow behind you while riding off-piste

b) Keeping speed

Reason b) means that parallel slalom racers aim for every turn to be a perfect carve.

NICOLIEN SAUERBREIJ

Born: 31 July 1979
From: Amsterdam, Netherlands
Job: Pro snowboarder

Sauerbreij won the **parallel giant slalom** at the 2010 Winter Olympics. This made her the first Dutch person ever to win a Winter Olympic medal for anything but ice skating.

BOARDERCROSS

Boardercross and snowboard cross are the same thing. Boardercross is the more common name, but snowboard cross is the name used at the Olympics. Whatever you call it, the thrills and spills of this type of race keep audiences on the edges of their seats.

Crashes and bashes

Boardercross races feature a group of riders (usually four) all starting together. They race side-by-side down the same course, through a series of **gates**. Inevitably, with the riders travelling at high speed and scrapping to get ahead of each other, crashes are common.

No Way!

The inventor of the snowboard cross format was Steve Rechtschaffner. He later went on to design the popular SSX series of video games.

Course design

Boardercross courses are designed to challenge every part of a snowboarder's skills. You have to be good at jumps and turns, steep sections and flat ones. And of course, you have to do all this while other riders are trying to do the same thing on the exact-same bit of snow.

gap jump

There are many different elements to a bordercross course. Riders try to carry plenty of speed into a gap jump, as it is much faster to jump between two ramps than ride over them.

Qualifying

Boardercross competitions start with qualifying. One at a time, each rider does a run down the course. The rider who sets the fastest time is ranked number one. The slowest rider gets the lowest ranking number. Qualifying is important because the rankings are used to position the riders in **heats**. A top ranking number will make it slightly easier to win your heat.

Racing

Heats are usually made up of four riders. When the starting signal goes off, everyone wants to get the **holeshot** – that means making it to the first turn in front of the others. That way, you can avoid people crashing into you, and hopefully slide safely down the course to victory. The first two riders to cross the finish line go through to the next round. This process continues until four riders are left: these are the finalists.

Riders bomb out of the start gates, crouched low for the best balance and the least air resistance.

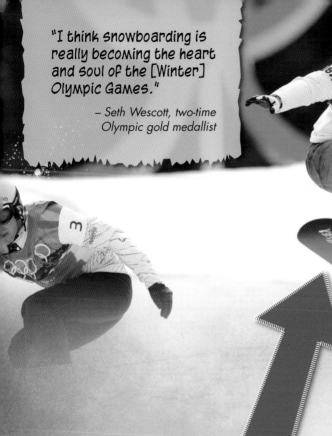

Snowboard cross at the Olympics

In 2006, "snowboard cross" appeared at the Winter Olympics for the first time. It was a massive hit with spectators. The competition was fresh and new compared to familiar sports such as ice dance and curling. Snowboard cross was so successful that at the next Winter Olympics, in 2010, a ski cross event was added to the programme.

SETH WESCOTT

Born: 28 June 1976
From: Maine, USA
Job: Pro snowboarder

Wescott won the first ever Olympic gold for snowboard cross in 2006. Then, in 2010, he managed to win gold again, despite starting the final in last place. Wescott steadily caught up, and managed to squeeze into first place on the very last jump.

19

PARALLEL GIANT SLALOM

Parallel giant slalom (usually called parallel GS) is the kind of snowboard racing that's closest to skiing. The racers do tight turns through a series of gates, aiming to get down the snaky course as fast as possible. Of course, this being snowboarding, they don't do it in the same way as ski racers!

PHILIPP SCHOCH

Born: 12 October 1979
From: Winterthur, Switzerland
Job: Pro snowboarder

Schoch was the first snowboarder to win two Olympic golds (2002, 2006). It was the first two times parallel giant slalom had ever been contested at the Olympics.

NO WAY!

Imagine having to beat your brother to win Olympic gold! That's just what happened to Philipp Schoch in the 2006 parallel GS final. Philipp got gold, older brother Simon silver.

Separated by fractions of a second, two racers carve down a parallel giant slalom course.

Side-by-side action

In parallel giant slalom there are two courses side-by-side. Two snowboarders start at the same moment, and the first across the finish line wins. They do this up to three times: the first racer to win twice goes through to the next round. The rounds continue until there are only two racers left in the competition. These two fight it out for first and second place.

The course

The two side-by-side courses are supposed to be exactly the same. However, this is practically impossible to achieve, so one side almost always ends up being slightly faster. The racers draw lots to decide who rides on which side. To even this out, they swap sides for the second descent, then back again for the third (if there is a third).

HALF-PIPE

Half-pipe is one of the most thrilling snowboard events to watch. The competitors launch spectacular airs, one after another. Everything happens in a tightly packed area, and the spectators are often very close to the riders.

The pipe

A half-pipe is almost exactly what it sounds like: a giant-sized half of a pipe, cut lengthways into the snow. The pipe has a flattened bottom and steep, quarter-circle sides. At the very tops, the walls of the half-pipe become **vertical**. Almost all half-pipes slope downhill. This makes it easier for the riders to keep as much speed as possible.

Parts of the half pipe are sprayed blue, so that the riders can see the edges and the curve of the slope.

lip

vertical section

A half-pipe run

Each run starts at the entry ramp, where the rider swoops down into the pipe. He or she then rides across the pipe and launches an aerial off the vertical section. One of the key skills in half-pipe is landing tricks smoothly enough to allow you to keep speed. Doing this means you can launch another big trick after your next **transition**.

Riders go back and forth across the pipe, **pulling** aerials and plants (a bit like a handstand) each time they hit the **lip**. The tricks get smaller further down the pipe, as the rider loses speed.

NAIL-BITING MOMENT!

In 2007, legendary Norwegian snowboarder Terje Haakonsen set the world record for the highest ever snowboard aerial. He jumped 9.8 metres (32 feet). That's clear over a giraffe that's standing on another giraffe's head!

KELLY BERGER

Born: 11 January 1996
From: Mammoth Lakes, USA
Job: Student and pro snowboarder

One to watch for the future! Berger won her first US Revolution Tour event on the half-pipe in Mount Snow in 2012, despite being just 16 years old.

Pushing the limits

Snowboarders are always pushing the limits. For example, a few years ago Shaun White invented a move called the double cork. What is a double cork? Ben Kilner, an Olympic competitor from Scotland, says: "It's kind of a twisting double backflip where you have to spin around at least three times."

Before the 2010 Winter Olympics, the double cork was thought so dangerous that some people suggested it should be banned. But just a year later, Torstein Horgmo (pictured below) landed the first ever TRIPLE cork, in a Big Air competition.

Superpipe

A superpipe is a giant version of a half-pipe. Riders started building them as part of their quest to push the limits and do increasingly difficult tricks. The extra speed the huge slopes of a superpipe create lets the rider go higher in the air. This gives him or her time to fit more moves into each aerial.

SHAUN WHITE

Born: 3 September 1986
From: San Diego, USA
Job: Pro snowboarder and skateboarder

Though also a top pro skateboarder, White is best known for snowboarding. Many people think he is the best snowboarder ever.

The list of Shaun White's achievements would fill a book. They include:

- First ever back-to-back X Games gold medal winner (2008, 2009)
- First ever winner of two Olympic half-pipe golds (2006, 2010)
- first-ever rider to win five superpipe Winter X Games gold medals in a row.

"If you're going off a 90-foot [27-metre] jump, you can't say: 'Oh, I don't want to do this now.' You're going, no matter what."

– Shaun White

SLOPESTYLE

Slopestyle contests take place in a limited area, surrounded by spectators who never know what trick they will see next. The riders do runs in a purpose-built park, aiming to include the highest, most difficult tricks possible.

The course

Slopestyle courses are usually based around a series of jumps. These come one after another, and are steep enough to allow the riders to launch massive aerials.

Tricks to look out for

Big aerials draw the biggest gasps from spectators. All the top riders can do spins and grabs. Some add spins to the flips, making it a "cork" (because they are twisting round like a corkscrew). Putting tricks such as these into a smooth, fast run will earn a top score.

Tignes Ski and Snowboard Resort in the Northern French Alps hosted the 2012 Winter X Games.

Competition format

Slopestyle competitions usually take place in two parts, qualifications and finals. In qualification, each rider does two runs. Their best run counts, and the riders with the highest scores reach the finals. Normally there are between 6 and 10 finalists. In the finals, each rider does two more runs. The highest score wins.

BREANNA STANGELAND

Born: 9 October 1988
From: Calgary, Canada
Job: Professional snowboarder
Stangeland started snowboarding to be like her super-cool brother. Winner of the 2011/12 World Snowboard Tour Slopestyle title, she is one of a crop of North American female slopestylers who are pushing the boundaries of women's snowboarding.

BIG AIR

Big Air contests are one of snowboarding's most spectacular formats. The riders launch terrifyingly huge aerials off some of the biggest ramps in snowboarding. Because these ramps can be built and covered in artificial snow anywhere cold, Big Air contests are sometimes held in cities. The biggest attract hundreds of thousands of spectators.

Austria's Michael Macho performs a spectacular aerial during the Snowboard Big Air FIS World Cup in Stockholm, Sweden in 2011.

The ramps

Big Air contests generally feature one or two giant ramps. Their only purpose is to launch the riders as high and fast as possible. The ramps can be 35 metres (115 feet) high or more. As they launch, the riders can be travelling at well over 65 kph (40 mph).

Contest format

Contest formats vary, but Big Air competitions are usually split into qualifying, semi-finals, and finals. In qualifying, everyone does two jumps. The four riders with the highest scores go through to the semi-finals. In these, each rider does three jumps. Only their highest score counts: the two who score best go through to the two-rider final.

> "The person that's influenced me the most is Torstein [Horgmo, see page 24], with his style and progressing the sport and keeping the focus on style."
>
> – Mark McMorris

MARK McMORRIS

Born: 9 December 1993
From: Regina, Canada
Job: Professional snowboarder
McMorris is most famous for being the first rider ever to land a **backside** triple cork 1440 in 2011. This is a trick in which the rider spins four times and flips over three times while in the air. In the backside version, the rider's spin faces his back downhill first.

JUDGING

In snowboard contests such as half-pipe, slopestyle, and Big Air, judges give each rider a score. The judges' scores are based on their overall impression of the run. The maximum score a rider can earn is either 10 or, more commonly, 100.

Each aerial and other trick count towards a rider's overall score.

Key elements in a judge's score

The judges are thinking about five key elements when they decide the overall score a run should be given:

1) *Execution* – did the rider land each trick? Were the transitions between tricks fast and smooth?

2) *Variety* – was a good variety of tricks included, or did the rider just do similar tricks for the whole run?

3) *Difficulty* – how hard were the tricks? Riders get higher scores if they do tricks that are rarely seen, or have never been done before.

4) *Use of **terrain*** – did the rider use the pipe/snow park/ramp to its maximum potential?

5) *Amplitude* – how high or long were the aerials?

NO WAY!

In 2012, Shaun White scored the first ever perfect superpipe score (100) in X Games history (see page 40). His run included a frontside double cork 1260 and a double McTwist 1260. Just trying to work out what those *are* is hard enough for most people!

Fairness

In any event, with human judges awarding scores, mistakes can be made. In snowboard contests, there are usually seven judges. In the interests of fairness, the highest and lowest scores are not used. This prevents over-scoring and under-scoring, and leaves five scores counting.

"Snowboarding is about ... doing it your own way and doing your best run ... [When] rules start telling you how to do your run, it [messes] things up."

– Kevin Pierce, pro snowboarder

EXTREME FREERIDE

Unlike lots of things that are called "extreme", these contests really *are* extreme. The riders navigate their way down a huge mountainside, littered with cliffs, rocks, narrow strips of snow, and other obstacles. Extreme freeride is for experts only! A panel of judges gives each run a score.

Pick your own line

There is no set course in an extreme freeride contest. The riders have to stay within a certain area, but within it they can pick their own route or **line**. Before they begin, each rider scans the competition area, looking for the best way down the mountainside. They aim to pick a line that allows them to show off their skills and impress the judges, but also to stay alive.

"I will try to do my best without breaking any bones!"

– Jonathon "Douds" Charlet, 2012 Freeride World Champion

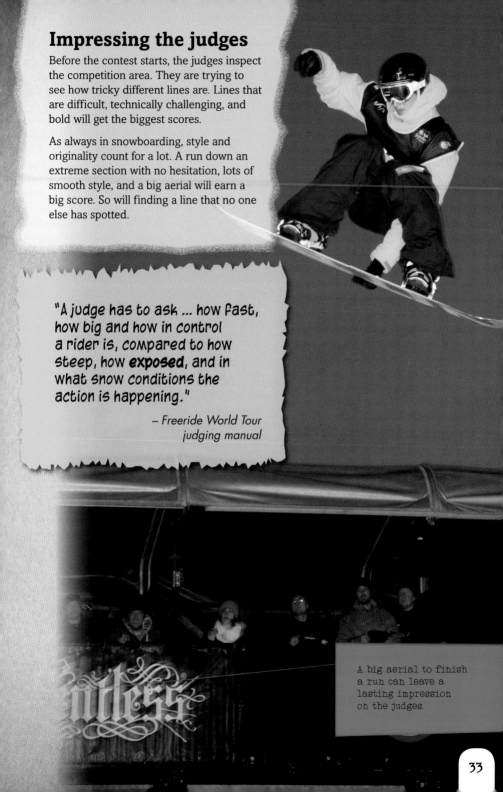

Impressing the judges

Before the contest starts, the judges inspect the competition area. They are trying to see how tricky different lines are. Lines that are difficult, technically challenging, and bold will get the biggest scores.

As always in snowboarding, style and originality count for a lot. A run down an extreme section with no hesitation, lots of smooth style, and a big aerial will earn a big score. So will finding a line that no one else has spotted.

"A judge has to ask ... how fast, how big and how in control a rider is, compared to how steep, how **exposed**, and in what snow conditions the action is happening."

– Freeride World Tour judging manual

A big aerial to finish a run can leave a lasting impression on the judges.

Big-mountain hotspots

The world's biggest big-mountain competitions take place in Europe and North America. They happen on slopes so challenging that few riders can even get down them, let alone show off their skills!

Revelstoke, Canada

Revelstoke has some extreme terrain right on its doorstep. To the east are the Selkirk Mountains and the wilds of the Glacier National Park. Visitors to Revelstoke are practically guaranteed **fat** powder. (That's a good thing – it means the snow is deep, wide, and particularly enjoyable!)

Kirkwood, USA

High in the Californian mountains, Kirkwood is well known for its challenging snowboarding terrain and deep snow.

Valdez, Alaska

Massive amounts of snow and endless mountains combine to make Valdez a must-visit destination for any travelling snowboarder. Each year the nearby Thompson Pass is home to the Tailgate Alaska event, a 12-day-long off-piste wilderness festival. This is also home to the annual World Freeride Championship.

Verbier, Switzerland

The off-piste here is so good that one of the lines is known as "Stairway to Heaven".

Chamonix-Mont Blanc, France

Nestled under Europe's highest mountain, Mont Blanc, Chamonix is home to some of the continent's most daring snowboarders.

Mont Blanc provides a stunning backdrop for the thousands of snowboarders who visit Chamonix every year.

JONATHAN CHARLET

Born: 10 June 1984
From: Chamonix, France
Job: pro snowboarder and mountain guide

Charlet, the 2012 World Champion, comes from Chamonix, France. It's one of Europe's most extreme snowboarding locations. He says that, here, "You have to know everything about snow and glaciers, if you don't want to die!"

"I love the mountains and any day I am on my snowboard is a good day!"

– Shannan Yates, extreme freerider

NO WAY!

The Pas de Chèvre route in Chamonix, France has a **vertical drop** of 1.5 kilometres (almost a mile)!

RAIL JAM

Rail jams are full of non-stop action. The tricks happen fast and furiously, so there's always something to see. Rail jams are popular with spectators as well as riders, and there can be thousands of people in the crowd.

The course

The course is small and simple. A short slope allows the riders to build up a bit of speed, and there is usually one main rail. The organizers sometimes put in one or two other obstacles – most often rails, but sometimes a box or wall as well. The course does not need a lot of space or snow, so rail jams sometimes take place in big cities. That way, the competition is guaranteed a good crowd.

Rail jams often take place in urban settings. A 30-metre rail jam course was constructed in Times Square, New York, USA in 2006.

Contest format

Rail jams usually go on for an hour. The riders take it in turns to do a run, and are allowed to do as many runs as possible within the hour. They are aiming for rides that combine high difficulty with smoothness and speed. The judges usually give prizes for Best Overall Performance, Best Male Trick, and Best Female Trick.

FOREST BAILEY

Born: 9 November 1991
From: Vermont, New England, USA
Job: pro snowboarder

Despite his young age, Forest has already earned a name for himself in the world of snowboarding. A keen skateboarder, he brings a skateboarding edge to his riding, and excels in street competitions. In 2012 he won gold in the Winter X Games Street final, and rounded off the year by winning the Burton Rail Days title in Tokyo.

SNOWBOARDING AT THE OLYMPICS

The Olympic Games is the world's biggest sports event. In the 1990s, snowboarding was the fastest-growing winter sport in the world. In 1998, the two came together for the first time, when snowboarding half-pipe and giant slalom appeared at the Winter Olympics.

A tricky start

Qualification to the Olympics was (and is) controlled by the **International Ski Federation (FIS)**, skiing's governing body. Many snowboarders thought the FIS was trying to muscle in on snowboarding's success, without having any understanding of the sport. As a result, top riders – including the world's best, Terje Haakonsen – **boycotted**, or refused to enter, the Games in 1998.

Snowboarding livens things up

As a new sport, snowboarding has been able to introduce lively new types of competition to the Winter Games. First, in 2002, GS was changed to parallel GS. Four years later, "snowboard cross" appeared for the first time and was a massive hit. The 2014 addition of slopestyle has added to the excitement. Some of these new formats have since been copied by skiing: ski cross first appeared in 2010, and ski half-pipe was added to the 2014 line-up.

"Why do [the International Olympic Committee] have a ski federation organize snowboarding events? I just decided not to go."

– Terje Haakonsen, on his Olympic boycott

TERJE HAAKONSEN

Born: 11 October 1974
From: Vinje, Norway
Job: Snowboarder

Haakonsen is so famous in snowboarding circles that you only have to use his first name, Terje, for people to know who you mean. His smooth style and skill at riding any terrain has influenced many of today's top riders. Terje led the boycott of snowboarding at the 1998 Winter Olympics.

OTHER CONTESTS

Around the world, there are snowboarding contests of all kinds. At one extreme, a bunch of friends build a kicker (small ramp) and see who can get furthest or highest jumping from it. At the other extreme are giant, week-long festivals of competition and fun.

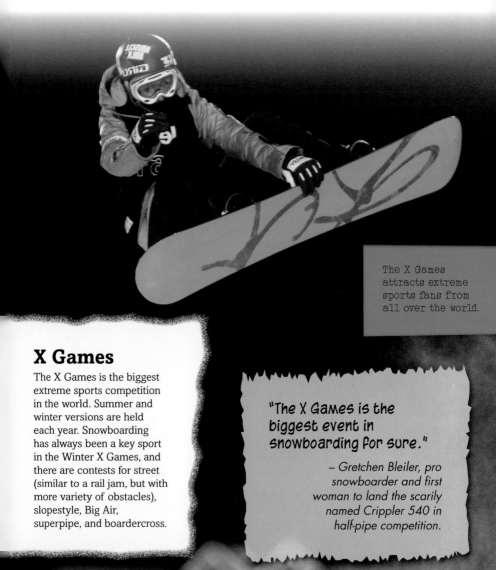

The X Games attracts extreme sports fans from all over the world.

X Games

The X Games is the biggest extreme sports competition in the world. Summer and winter versions are held each year. Snowboarding has always been a key sport in the Winter X Games, and there are contests for street (similar to a rail jam, but with more variety of obstacles), slopestyle, Big Air, superpipe, and boardercross.

"The X Games is the biggest event in snowboarding for sure."

– Gretchen Bleiler, pro snowboarder and first woman to land the scarily named Crippler 540 in half-pipe competition.

Canada's Sebastien Toutant catches huge air in an Air and Style contest in Munich, Germany in 2011.

MUNICH 2011   MUNICH 2011

air style

World Tours

In the last few years, some of the top snowboard contests have joined together to make up a Snowboard World Tour. The points riders win at each contest are added up at the end of the season. Whoever has most points wins the world tour title. There is also a separate Freeride World Tour, for big-mountain snowboarders.

SNOWBOARD CONTESTS

There are lots of big snowboard contests. The main ones include:

* *Air and Style, Innsbrück, Austria*: this Big Air competition attracts huge crowds every year

* ***Snowdome** Jam, Tokyo, Japan*: unusual because it is held indoors, but still packed with top snowboarders

* *Shakedown, Mont Sant-Saveur, Canada*: a chilled-out event that aims to promote snowboarding. It combines Big Air with rail jam, and the riders go when they are ready, rather than in a particular order. This relaxed format is so successful that Shakedowns now also take place in the United States and Europe.

QUIZ

1. You are in a lift queue waiting to catch a drag lift, and the attendant asks if you are regular or goofy foot. You answer:

a) I'm perfectly OK, thank you.

b) Goofy, left-foot at the back OR Regular, right foot at the back.

c) How dare you?! I always walk like this.

2. A friend offers you some free tickets to a Big Air competition. What is your first thought?

a) Some sort of crazy farting contest? Great!

b) Excellent! Maybe I'll see a real-live triple cork aerial!

c) How dare you?! So what if my hair needs a trim?
I'm growing it out.

3. What's the most exciting thing you can imagine waking up to on a snowboarding trip?

a) Fresh croissants! And bacon! And pancakes!

b) A fresh dump of deep powder snow.

c) How dare you?! Why would I be sleeping on a snowboarding trip?

4. You forget to fasten your snow skirt before going out. What is the worst that could happen?

a) My whole outfit will be simply ruined without that skirt, darling! I'd never be able to show my face at that resort again.

b) I fall over and slide down the slope on my bottom, gathering a large amount of snow up the back of my jacket. Brrrr!

c) How dare you?! I'm a gentleman, and would NEVER wear a skirt.

5. Your grandfather tells you he has an old Snurfer in his attic, which you are welcome to have a go on. How do you respond?

a) Shrug in a confused way; say, I hope your cold gets better soon, Grandad.

b) A piece of snowboarding history! I don't know whether to ride it or hang it on a wall.

c) Grandad, how dare you?! I outgrew those silly blue children's toys years ago.

6. You are watching a superpipe contest on TV, and the commentator says someone has just taken off on his backside. Your reaction is:

a) Amazing! It's hard enough when you take off on your feet – that guy must be *really* good.

b) Wow – most people find that the hardest direction to spin. Good trick!

c) How dare he?! Everyone's trying their hardest, there's no need to be rude.

7. A friend tells you they did the Pas de Chevre ('step of the goats') route in Chamonix, France, last winter. You think:

a) Why would you want to go for a walk with a bunch of goats?

b) You must be fitter than I thought to have managed a vertical drop of 1.5 kilometres.

c) How dare you?! I always pass the salt and pepper when asked!

8. You are invited to compete in a boardercross competition. What do you think?

a) I love my own country, thank you, I don't need to cross any borders.

b) Great, it will spur me on to practise my jumps and turns.

c) How dare you?! I love snowboarding, it never makes me cross.

How did you do?

Mostly a) – you must be one of those people who flicks through books starting at the back. Better to read it first, then do the quiz.

Mostly b) – excellent, you must be a keen snowboarder and a good reader.

Mostly c) – firstly, calm down, and take a couple of deep breaths. Maybe drink a glass of water. Next, you probably ought to get your hearing and eyesight tested!

GLOSSARY

aerial jump trick in which a snowboarder leaves the ground

backside the rider's spin faces his back downhill first

bindings equipment for attaching feet to a board, allowing control and security. Bindings have made sports such as water-skiing, wakeboarding, kitesurfing, and snowboarding possible.

boycotted refused to attend

breathable allowing the moisture released by people's skin when they sweat to pass through

exposed especially dangerous, with possible deadly consequences if you fall

fat deep, wide, and particularly enjoyable

flip turn end over end, like a circus acrobat

gate two markers placed on a snowboard course, between which racers have to pass. Missing a gate means you are disqualified.

gilet sleeveless top, usually with a high neck, which adds warmth but not bulk to an outfit

goofy snowboarding (or surfing, kiteboarding, or skateboarding) with your right foot forward

grab trick in which a snowboarder grabs the rail, nose, or tail of the board

grind skateboarding name for what snowboarders call a jib (to slide along a rail or other platform while riding a snowboard)

heat single round or race within a bigger competition

heel edge edge of a snowboard behind a rider's feet

holeshot first place at the first turn on a boardercross course. Everyone wants the holeshot, as it means they have a clear run at the rest of the course.

International Ski Federation (FIS) Fédération Internationale de Ski; world governing body for skiing and snowboarding

line path chosen by a snowboarder on his or her way down the slope. Almost everyone sees and rides a slightly different line, depending on their skill level, how they are feeling, and the type of snowboarding they prefer.

lip sharp top edge of a ramp or slope. In a half-pipe, the lip is the top of the pipe's sidewall.

off-piste away from prepared ski or snowboard runs

parallel giant slalom snowboard competition in which two riders race down separate, identical courses side by side

powder snow that has not been bashed down to make a hard-packed surface. Most snowboarders love to ride through fresh powder, though this is much harder than it looks.

pull perform or complete

regular snowboarding (or surfing, kiteboarding, or skateboarding) with your left foot forward

run single, non-stop journey down a slope

skate move a snowboard forward with your back foot freed from the bindings, by pushing off against the snow with it, like a skateboarder

snowdome indoor snowboarding location, with a controlled temperature and artificial snow. The world's largest snowdome is, surprisingly, in Dubai.

spin pivot or turn quickly sideways, like a spinning top

switch backward, with the tail of the board in front

terrain area of land and the character of its physical features, such as woods, valleys, hills, and slopes

toe edge edge of a snowboard toward which a rider's feet point

transition gap between one trick and another. In a half-pipe, the transition happens between one sidewall of the pipe and the other

vertical straight up and down

vertical drop difference in height between the top and bottom of a run

FIND OUT MORE

Books

Adrenaline Rush: Snowboarding, Yvonne Thorpe (Smart Apple Media, 2012)

Extreme Snowboarding (Sports on the Edge!), Daniel Benjamin (Marshall Cavendish Children's Books, 2011)

Snowboarding the World (Footprint Travel Guides), Matt Barr, Chris Moran and Ewan Wallace (Footprint Handbooks, 2006)

Snowboarding (World Sports Guide), Paul Mason (A&C Black, 2011)

Websites

whitelines.mpora.com
The online presence of Europe's leading snowboard magazine, this is a great place to pick up news about competition results, rider interviews, trick tips, and even rider reviews of some of the world's leading resorts.

www.worldsnowboardguide.com
This is a web resource based on the popular travel guide. You can look up particular resorts by name, search by country, or just browse the guide's recommendations. The resort guides are reasonably detailed, and include information about how suitable each resort is for beginners and particular types of snowboarding.

www.worldsnowboardtour.com
This is the home page of the international World Snowboard Tour, with news of where to watch events, results, and rider profiles.

www.freerideworldtour.com
There is plenty of information here about extreme freeride competitions, from the organizing body of the world tour. The section on juniors has helpful advice on how to get into this most extreme snowboard discipline safely. There's also a "Riders' Diary" section, where you can read what it's like to be a promising junior big-mountain rider.

DVDs

Decade: The Snowboard Progression of 1998

Right at the top of most people's lists of the best snowboard films ever made, *Decade* has it all: star riders, extreme locations, and some groundbreaking tricks.

The Haakonsen Factor

A classic film, featuring the coolest cat in snowboarding in his prime, with action spanning Norway, New Zealand, Alaska, and the Rocky Mountains. Even today, the fluidity of Haakonsen's riding is sometimes astonishing. The soundtrack is another highlight.

Neverland

Shot in the game-changing winter of 2010/11, this movie has some of the best off-piste sequences ever caught on film.

Top snowboarding spots

Verbier, Valais, Switzerland

You might find yourself sharing the cable car with a minor European royal at this very fancy resort. The hard-core snowboarders are here for the famous off-piste runs, which are only rivalled in Europe by the Austrian resort of St Anton.

Chamonix, Haute Savoie, France

One of Europe's oldest mountain towns is home to some of the most extreme riding in the continent, bar none. Described by the writer Mark Twain as the, "death sports capital of the world", Chamonix really is for advanced riders only!

Stowe Mountain, Vermont, USA

At the heart of the US East Coast snowboard scene, Stowe occupies a special place in the hearts of many snowboarders. The nearby town of Burlington is home to Burton, the world's biggest snowboard company.

Whistler, British Columbia, Canada

There is something for everyone at Whistler, from beginners to experts. The snow is dry and deep, and guaranteed to be good every winter.

INDEX